D0732194

Gallery Books
Editor: Peter Fallon

THE ROSE-GERANIUM

Eiléan Ní Chuilleanáin

The Rose-Geranium

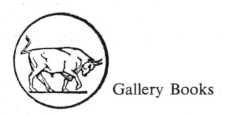 Gallery Books

The Rose-Geranium
is first published
simultaneously in paperback
and in a clothbound edition
in July 1981.

The Gallery Press
19 Oakdown Road
Dublin 14
Ireland.

© Eiléan Ní Chuilleanáin

All rights reserved

Cover design by Michael Kane

ISBN 0 904011 23 2 (clothbound)
0 904011 24 0 (paperback)

Acknowledgements
Acknowledgements are due to the editors and publishers of *Aquarius, Bananas, City Views, Cyphers, The Gorey Detail, Plough-shares* (Mass.), *Poetry Ireland Review, The Writers: A Sense of Ireland* (O'Brien Press) and of Wake Forest University Press (North Carolina) who have published some of these poems.
The Gallery Press gratefully acknowledges the assistance of An Chomhairle Ealaíon (The Arts Council of Ireland) towards the publication of this book.

Contents

Night Journeys

There are more changes each time I return

Two widows are living together in the attic
Among the encyclopaedias
And gold vestments.
        A fishmonger
Opens his shop at the angle of the stairs.

The scullery I see has been extended,
A wide cloister, thatched, with swallows
Nesting over windows, now hides the garden.

I wake in Rome, and my brother, aged fifteen, meets me.
My father has sent him with a naggin of coffee and brandy,
which I drink on the platform.

And wake again in an afternoon bed
Grey light sloping from window-ledge
To straw-seated armchair. I get up,
Walk down a silent corridor
To the kitchen. Twilight and a long scrubbed table,
The tap drips in an enamel basin
Containing peeled potatoes. A door half-open and
I can hear somebody snoring.

Cork

1.
The island, with its hooked
Clamps of bridges holding it down,
Its internal spirals
Packed, is tight as a ship
With a name in Greek or Russian on its tail:

As the river, flat and luminous
At its fullest, images the defences:
Ribbed quays and stacked roofs
Plain warehouse walls as high as churches
Insolent flights of steps.

Encamped within, the hurried exiles
Sheltering against the tide
A life in waiting,
Waking reach out for a door and find a bannister,
Reach for a light and find their hands in water,
Their rooms all swamped by dreams.
In their angles the weeds
Flourish and fall in a week,
Their English falters and flies from them,
The floods invade them yearly.

2.

In the graveyards of the city, wells
                    of arrested sound,
The tombstones are swaying like a house of cards.

The night obscures them as the evergreens obscure
Tablets fixed on their boundary walls,

They are shouldered by tall square houses
Chimneys nodding to each other
Over the heads of gesturing
Angels, all back and no sex.

3.
A slot of air, the snug
Just wide enough for the door to open
And bang the knees of everyone inside;
You face a window blank with dust
Half-inch spiderwebs
Rounding the squares of glass
And a view on either hand of mirrors
Shining at each other in the gloom.

A woman's head, bowed
A glint on her forehead
Obliquely seen leaning on the counter
At the end of a vista of glasses
And one damp towel.

And out of sight in the cellars
Spinning in the dust
The spiders are preparing for autumn.
They weave throughout the city:
Selecting the light for their traps,
They swell with darkness.

4.
Missing from the scene
The many flat surfaces,
Undersides of doors, of doormats
Blank backs of wardrobes
The walls of tunnels in walls
Made by wires of bells, and the shadows of square spaces
Left high on kitchen walls
By the removal of those bells on their boards,

The returning minotaur pacing transparent
In the transparent maze cannot
Smell out his stall; the angles all move towards him,
No alcove to rest his horns.
At dawn he collapses in the garden where
The delicate wise slug is caressing
Ribbed undersides of blue cabbage leaves
While on top of them rain dances.

As the fog descends,
'What will I do in winter?', he thinks
Shocked by the echoing blows
Of logs unloading in courtyards
Close by, on every side.

5.

When you pass the doorway
You are going underground: it is light and warm
And nothing is as you expected.
A table laid since breakfast-time,
Cake and sherry, with whiskey for the men.

Outside the window it is Sunday
But the neighbours' washing hangs on the line
And between the stiff squares of white cloth
Just visible, a glass window,
Blackness beyond
Half veiled by a net curtain,
A lined curtain, a lampshade
The wooden back of a looking-glass, then blackness.

We could be in any city.

6. A Gentleman's Bedroom

Those long retreating shades,
A river of roofs inclining
In the valley side. Gables and stacks
And spires, with trees tucked between them:
All graveyard shapes
Viewed from his high windowpane.

A coffin-shaped looking-glass replies,
Soft light, polished, smooth as fur,
Blue of mown grass on a lawn,
With neckties crookedly doubled over it.

Opening the door, all walls point at once to the bed
Huge red silk in a quarter of the room
Knots drowning in deep mahogany
And uniform blue volumes shelved at hand.

And a desk calendar, a fountain-pen,
A weighty table-lighter in green marble,
A cigar-box, empty but dusted,
A framed young woman in a white dress
Indicate the future from the cold mantel.

The house sits silent,
The shiny linoleum
Would creak if you stepped on it.
Outside it is still raining
But the birds have begun to sing.

7.
The shopfront says HARDWARE, and above it
A long dusty lace curtain
Blows out of a window.
A grey-haired woman and a small girl
Are leaning out, and I look up at them
Like a fish putting its head up
To get a better view of a heron
But I can't see into the room.
They lean out to listen to the soft notes
The brass band marching away from them
Downhill to the quays.
In the street, the children have all gone after the band
And the women are still silent
Still pausing from their counters and shopping-bags.

8.
The lizard, heavy-shouldered,
With long tail, stood, head raised
Straddling from corner to corner
A flat lettered stone.

I see him once more as I look
Down over the muscular back
Of a small brown river vanishing
In an arched tunnel.

With a low chirp a sparrow dives
Between two stones of the arch

Cold wind rattles the stacks
Flings the smoke abroad:
Confraternity banners:
Cold wind and silence.

9.
Geometry of guilt, the windows
Broken or always empty:
Daylight sucked in and lost, a bird astray:

The knife edge of the street, blinded
Fronts of houses like a bacon-slicer
Dropping to infinity, down

Draughty quays and frozen bridges
And the façades are curves of seeping stone
As damp as a scullery

Or a child's game of windows and doors arranged
Matching the caves of womb and skull.
Inside, only the long drop: vacant pillars

Frame only one sound from the inhabited past:
Gentle voices of a brass band,
Open-air, midsummer, soft as a poppy.

10. *Géarsmacht na mBradán*

Imprisoned here, not daring
To peep above the shadow
Line where the air presses down,

It is dark, and then a break
Of light, cold and shrill, bubbles
And the shining salmon, with

Their crooked jaws, flattening
The weeds with a bow wave, slide
Over us like the morning.

We see the rocks about us and their peaks and ruts
Until the weeds wave gently back and enclose us.
The water is bitter to us
As we wait for their return.

11.
Late on a summer evening
The houses are parting with heat
And the streets are warm
As a bedroom full of sleeping children.

The wheels of a car, a dull
Even sound, as if it drove on a carpet
Among the cracked pavements
And the painted windowsills on which
Lamplit people are sitting and talking.

We are soft-footed and busy as dogs
Disappearing down alleyways,
The faces I meet are warped with meaning.

We turn away from each other,
Our shoulders are smooth as the plaster veils of statues
That are turning their backs in the windows and doors.

12.
The crazy houses, walls as soft as cake
Built by an old bridge or on a stream
(A cellar door with a boat pointing tideward
And floods on the stairway in September and March)

Crazed lethal machinery spanning inlets:
Beams and rafters light with age: you showed me
The murdered distilleries that mark the streams.

They persist underground and slope alongside blank walls,
The high stacks have crumbled.

The water bubbles through gratings, the slates loosen and crash,
The flats of water in flooded streets
Are dancing, bouncing with rain.

The Duke of Marlborough, the Black and Tans . . .

Shopfronts now reduced to a man's height,
The mark of fire and water
Still stamped black on paint and plaster.

13. *Sandstone*
The soft rock that foils the maker
That splinters in wavering faces
In layers of broken light
Colour of the patched river:

Even in the gravel on the shore
Where bone and glass are schemed
Contoured to a flattened eggshape
This one wears to roughness.

It cannot forget the alleyways within
Their weaknesses, their coastlines impose.

Ridged north and south it hunches
Around the city
Arrogant as the intersecting
Lines on the compass disk.

Four Poems

Séamus Murphy, died 2nd October 1975

Walking in the graveyard, a maze
Of angels and families
The path coils like a shaving of wood
We stop to read the names.

In time they all come around
Again, the spearbearer, the spongebearer
Ladder and pillar
Scooped from shallow beds.

Carrying black clothes
Whiskey and ham for the wake
The city revolves
White peaks of churches clockwise lifting and **falling.**

The hill below the barracks
The sprouting sandstone walls go past
And as always you are facing the past
Finding below the old clockface

The long rambles of the spider
In the narrow bed of a saint
The names inscribed travelling
Into a winter of stone.

The Last Glimpse of Erin

The coastline, a swimmer's polished shoulder heaving
On the edge of sky: our eyes make it grow:
The last glimpse, low and smooth in the sea.

We face the air, all surfaces become
Sheer, one long line is growing
Like a spider's navel cord: the distance

From your low shoulder lost in the quilt,
An arm thrown forward: a swimmer: your head
Buried in a pillow like a wave.

The white light skirting the cloud pierces
Glass riddled with small scratches and creates
The depths and cadences of a spider's web.

A man is holding his baby and laughing,
He strokes her cheek with a brownstained finger
While his wife sews a wristbutton on his other hand.

The island trimmed with waves is lost in the sea,
The swimmer lost in his dream.

"He Hangs in Shades the Orange Bright"

So quiet the girl in the room
                    he says
It is a precarious bowl
Of piled white eggs on a high shelf

Against the dark wardrobe the gleam
Of skin and the damp hair inclining
Over her leaning shoulder fades
Into dark. She leans on a hand
Clutching the bedrail, her breasts pale
Askew as she stands looking left
Past the window towards the bright glass.
But from the window it is clear
That the dark glass reflects nothing;
Brilliance of the water-bottle
Spots the ceiling

The man in the courtyard waters the roots of the trees
And birds in their cages high on the red wall sing.

She moves her head and sees
The window tall on hinges
Each oblong tightly veiled. One side admits
Air through a grey slatted shutter, and light
Floats to the ceiling's
Profound white lake.

Still the sound of water and the stripe
Of blue sky and red wall,
Dark green leaves and fruit, one ripe orange
                              she says
The sheet lightning over the mountains
As I drove over the quiet plain
Past the dark orange-groves.

March 18th 1977

Waking with a sore head
A freshly bruised shin,
Forgetting the collision:
Eyes open and see
With relief, my coat on a hanger.

The early light that slants
Warm from the curtain illuminates
The skin of your face,
Glittering all over like a lake in a light wind—
The eyelids, those fine
Horizontal folds: like cliffs by a lake
Layered and loaded with flowers.

When my skin was as smooth as
A jamjar of water
I looked for time in my father's eyes:
Brown and green circling,
A bead of yellow under the corner
When no part of my body
Was more private than a fish
Going round and round in a jamjar of water.

The Rose-Geranium

Like One Borne Away in a Dance and Veiled

She learned again so soon
How the body is subdued
To all the laws that rule
The acorn's fall and the erosion of tall cliffs.

Like one borne away in a dance and veiled
She dreamed of a high house with shining floors
Where they squatted over stoves
And well-shod women held breath in the lift
If ever they went out or in.

They chewed into the side of the tower,
A fungus. From the night-time street
The rooms they had invaded showed—
Their half-light, their droning seeped.

And the day the building fell into the street
And blood fell and bodies folded and spun
The prisoner had company:

X-ray bones of snow.
Rivers grinding south,
Planes of ice bleeding at the edges downstream.

2.
Alone I walk in a wood above Holyoke:
The white birch faces me, a peeled dead look,
Moonlit matt affronting the morning.

My skin is growing again, in air
Warm like a quilt. The trees
Are as close as a friend and a bottle.

Roadside gravel displays floodwater grooves,
A drift of wrappers thrown from machines.
Girdled with rust a white stone
Is unveiled among the husks, washed clean.

In the sky a pod full of people
Roars east to Boston.

3.
When she opened the egg the wise woman had given her,
she found inside some of her own hair and a tooth, still
bloody, from her own mouth.

One summer after another
The shore advanced and receded
As the boat shoved past the islands.

Dark bushy hills revolved in the path;
                                    and in each
Of the solid still rooms above bars,
                              the first sight
Caught at an angle, the glass questioning your face.

4.

'A l'usage de M. et Mme van Gramberen'
—the convent phrase (nothing is to be mine,
Everything ours) marks the small round enclosure,
Its table and bench. Distinguished
From the other old people, from the nuns' gravel
They sat in the windmill's afternoon shadow, half
Hidden by a moving carthorse's huge blond rump
And quarrelled over their sins for Saturday:
Examination of Conscience before Confession

Prepared and calm in case one thought
Struck them both, an attentive pose
Eluding me now, at ten in the morning, alone
With a clean college pantry: piled rings
Of glass rising, smooth as a weir.

The moment sways
Tall and soft as a poplar
Pointing into a lifetime of sky.

5.

The precious dry rose-geranium smell
Comes down with spirals of sunlit dust
From the high sill: nodding stems
Travelling out from the root
Embrace a fistful of dusk among the leaves.

The man sitting below, his head
Veiled in smoke, the face a cliff in shadow,
Waits: the sun in Scorpio climbs in
Dodging the fragrant leaves; and as subtly
As the eyes of two musicians touching
Light strokes his hair in place.

In spite of your long horizontal twilights
There is an instant when the sun meets the sea
Dividing light from dark
An hour when the shadow passes the mark on the wall
And the cloud of the rose-geranium dulls your hair.

6. *Waters Below*

From braided and trapped hills
The steam, rising,
Falling, sifts and follows
Creepers draped in the cleft
With flicker and drip, distilling;

And radiant in the dam,
Soft parallels dissolving cows,
It waits to plunge in freezing dark
Past scars of growth, longing for the gutter.

It ravishes, knowing no seed,
Handles and loses earth.

I look out on darkness and walls that move away,
I am seen, I reflect the starlight, but blinded
I seek for depths as planets fly from the sun,
What holds me in life is flowing from me and I flow
Falling, out of true.

Not portable as swallows,
Cleopatra's needle
Or fungus coating
Spirals of the body—

Or blossom split from the fallen plum-tree
Reaching stiffly aloft in a pint glass
Where the water chases its tail
Wishing to fall, and still falling.

7.
Light glancing along a public-house table
Stamps rings of glass like the circles
Left on water as the pebble skips.

It catches on your hands
Reaching at me from sleeves;
Your face shaded . . .

The head upright
Vertical bones
Eyebrows level,
Stiffening, that
Image I see when I please . . .

Grace, the instant overloaded, the spine
Righting itself, treading water. A boy
Makes tea, leaning over the sink, his weight
Landed on one foot, riding—
That seahorse backbone, ruffled at the hip,
The breeze lifting, filling cloth . . .

Sloping westward, the roads
Of the body, drumlin shoulder,
Away from sight the legs angled
Like dry wood scaffolding
Overgrown and left behind.
I lie down
And start work with the ivy.

8. *Cat in the Fishmarket*

The fishmarket, empty
At night, is locked.
The street warm, raining;
The restaurant doors
Open on the marketplace
Wide, catching cool air.

We watch her from our bright table
Through the conversation of workmen at their meal.

She dives in under
The high broken doors,
Returning soon after—
She can't have found much
Under those damp counters.
She runs in the rain

Seeing only feet and legs, undersides
Of doors, the empty stalls of night.

9.

As if suddenly reincarnated
One lunch-hour as Saint
Sebastian, pierced and visible,
The weathercock loses his freedom to turn,
Crowds advance on him like the four winds.

And in the street, under
Transparent branches of trees
Single, fixed, waving softly,
Human figures wave their transparent hands.

Down to the roots not a pocket, a closet
Not a ledge of them hidden.
As they pass the fairground they revolve
And the roundabouts waver, lifting and falling.

In a line from the crossroads, beyond
The fountain and the gentlemen's lavatory,
The road at infinity appears to curve a little
As a branch in summer weighed down by the young fruit.

Although raised up, steady, he can't be sure.
The scene pierces him with claws like a lobster's,
And somewhere an eye sees him as a whirlpool of glass.

10. *Waters Between*

Gazing in the cold at the bright scene
I reach to stroke the pane revealing the garden;
And it melts at my touch into a wall
Where a thousand silver drops are turning, turning away.

11.
In my dream I feel the shock of waking:
By the pillow, shadows of high branches,
Black rind and pale flower
Are signals from a garden drowned behind glass.
But between them, slipped alongside
Suburban Ranelagh, a narrow slice of land
Bears a fragile deck-cargo,
A small Protestant graveyard.

Lawn stumbles downhill over tombstones
(Roots of yew heave at the gravel path)
From the door of a low plain church;
And a black noticeboard, roofed for the rain,
Lettered in gold, stands sharply out
Against my decaying brick wall
More beautiful than the peartree's
Crowded black branches.

12.
So rarely we lie
As then, in darkness
A vertical gleam relieved
Where the brilliance from outside
Struck the glass over the hearth

(Breast high, if one stood,
Night lapped the bookshelves
And a dying light floated
Above us, never reaching
Us, our arrested embrace)

I think at once of
That amphibious
Twilight, now that the year is
Revisiting the spring shrine.
At my window the sharp, grey

Rectangles of stone
Range, parade in squares.
February light
Spreading across the walls over my head
Washes my room with shadows, cold until morning.

13.
The bones wake up, reach
Like tendrils for support
They feel the air in their cavities
Thunder of racehorses comes to them in the earth.

And, lightly rising, they climb aloft on her shoulders.
At once her own bones are reminded—it is the same,
The pressure—the rim of the clavicle biting
As the long humerus idly swings by her side.

Empty as a diagram
The laughable straight lines
Even now hold secrets
Of pleasure and fatigue. She sleeps,
Her head in the dish of a pelvis:
She knows how they stir beneath her.

14. *Talking to the Skin*

Screening the piled
Loose knitting, slopes
Gorges, fences,
What leagues apart,
The eye pierces
A grid, selects:

Skin, a sardine fisher's
Net shaken to dry
In a breeze, waves gleaming back.

With a twitch tides change,
The dark flag bangs against a sunset wind.
Another window spreads:

Talking to the light that scatters on the skin,
The sun drags its web on over the ocean face
Like a memory giving back nothing but knots of brightness.
The flaw muscling with light
Creases, darkens, bubbles in tears, arrives.

15.
Linked by precious chains
The feathered shapes moved with her as she moved,
Still descending lava stairs
Between scrub and a scatter
Of pines waving on the slope.
The command was, not to look
Down, but she did and saw the shore:

An oval sea, with the gleam
Of an iron lid raised an instant,
The rough pebbles where no boat rested
Or wave stirred among the weed.

And beyond the inlet, beyond the stiff black trees
That circle the burnt-out island,
Still flying, nesting, the slim grey birds
Without a cry, those birds of whom
No history of shapes transformed
Or grief outlived is ever told.
They flourish there, by the subterranean sea.

16.
Because this is the age of his life
In retrospect he will name theirs
He calls now at noon to feed their cats;
And stretched on a chaise longue in the clean house
He bites one of the yellow sweet apples
Wrinkling in the dish, while the female
Noses his feet. The black cat watches him
From the padded rail at his elbow:
A short demanding stare;
                               he recalls
A hand that shut off day,
An eye so close to what it sought, half-blinded,
A collage of hair and upholstery.

Beyond the half-drawn curtain, past the trailing boughs
Of their proper domain,
A goldfinch lights up
Childhood's cramped retreats,
Covenants made in
The scarce blood of berries
That dry on the twig.

The cats his shortlived witnesses.

17. *Amelia*

Remembering her half-sister Amelia, that girl
Whose hips askew made every step seem upstairs
The woman at the airport tells me that from her
One spring she bought the first small car.

After that it was trains and taxis for Amelia
For years and years, while the younger lay
In the car in a leafy mews in Dublin
Making love to a bald actor
Her elbow tightening
Linked through the steering-wheel.

She tells me, this hot noisy afternoon,
That Amelia now drives a car like a cabin-cruiser
In Halifax, Nova Scotia, where her husband
Fishes for lobster in short ice-free summers.

18.
I run my hand along the clean wood
And at once I am stroking the heads
Of everyone in the room.
                            Looking into the grain
Wavered and kinked like hairlines, what I see
Is the long currents of a pale ocean
Softly turning itself inside out.

Palm slack as air's belly touching the sea—
I feel the muscles tugging
In the wood, shoals hauling.

I look in vain for that boat
Biting its groove to the south-east,
For that storm, the knot of blindness
That left us thrashing
In steel corridors in the dark.

Beyond the open window
Along the silkpacked alleys of the souq
Momentary fountains and stairways
      (My hands move over the table
      Feeling the spines of fish and the keels)
I look, and fail, in the street
Searching for a man with hair like yours.